Truly Beautiful

A five week topical study focusing on key truths from the Book of Ephesians

Study Lessons

A Word from the Author

"It's God who see the beauty in everything, I just choose to agree with Him."

Sweet Pea - Veggie Tales

Sweet Pea got it right; she chose to agree with God! My prayer for you as you journey through the next five weeks in this study is that you will agree with Sweet Pea and see yourself the way God sees you.

Every day as you awake and stare into the mirror of God's Word, you will discover just how "truly beautiful" you are and that your Creator made you beautiful for HIM!

As a writer, author and biblical counselor, my heart is often stirred to teach on what I see coming through my counseling sessions. God called me to write this study as I witnessed many women, young and old, suffering from a lack of understanding of who they are in Christ.

Jesus often used the word "truly" to preface profound biblical truths He wanted us to take a hold of. I can't think of anything that is more crucial to the foundation of the Christian woman's life as her position in Christ – she must know that she is not just "beautiful" but "Truly Beautiful."

It has been said the Christian life is the becoming of "who you are" in Christ. My heart is that God would use this study in your life to help you embrace and live in the reality that you are His masterpiece. My hope is that you would walk confidently into the unique purpose and plan He has designed just for you!

Praying for you!

Margy Hill

Week 1

The Beauty Battle

Defining the Problem

You Are My True Beauty

Your real beauty is a work of art – hand carved by Me.

I have given you beautiful lips to speak words of life, beautiful eyes to see Me in everything, beautiful hands to help those in need, and a beautiful face to reflect My love to the world. I know you don't see yourself the way I do because you compare yourself to beauty idols that will soon be forgotten.

I will work wonders that will radiate true beauty from within. And when my work is completed, your character will show off my craftsmanship, and your beauty marks will be remembered by all that were loved by you.

Love,

Your Radiant King

Sheri Rose Shepherd

Week 1
Day 1

The Enemy of Beauty

For so many of us, embracing our God-given beauty and value is a life long struggle. Whether we are eight or eighty, we want to fit in; we want to be accepted, and we want to be beautiful. We are bombarded daily with billboards, fashion magazines and media that generate false messages about beauty. But because our battle with beauty goes deeper than what the eye can see, we are susceptible to the lies that come against what it means to be, *"truly beautiful"*.

Who is behind the lies about beauty? Is it the culture? Is it the airbrushed supermodels and the fashion industry? Is it the billion dollar diet craze and plastic surgery phenomena? Though these influences contribute to the fight, we must recognize our real enemy. His name is Satan.

What does Satan gain by attacking our perception of beauty and worth?

Those answers can be found in God's Word with a little bit of history on Satan. He is no stranger to the allure of beauty; in fact, Ezekiel describes him as "perfect in beauty". But that beauty became his downfall and the consequences of his pride got him thrown out of heaven. His splendor led to rebellion and he has been wreaking havoc ever since. His goal is to destroy the image of God in man and he ruthlessly seeks to come against women to twist and pervert the truths about beauty. You need only look at the outer ravaged body of a woman with anorexia to know that the lies she has believed in her heart are destroying her. Or the young woman who has scars all over her body from the cuts of a razor blade that were meant to dull the inner pain she could not handle.

Satan knows all too well that if he gets a woman to buy into the lies about beauty, she will soon find herself disappointed, depressed and eventually destroyed.

For this reason it is important that we discover God's truth. That we see ourselves as God sees us, for it is in His truth that we come to know and believe that we are *"truly beautiful"*.

Today's Beauty Truth

To be truly beautiful is to see yourself as God sees you.

Apply it to Your Life

To help you better grasp today's lesson, read Ezekiel 28:11-17. Though the passage is referring to the King of Tyre, the Scripture is also speaking to the evil one working in his life. God is giving us a picture of Satan and his fall from the garden.

1. Write out Ezekiel 28:17. How does this help you understand why Satan's main attack is towards a woman's beauty and her appearance?

2. How is it easy for a woman's heart to be "lifted" up because of her beauty?

3. We quickly see the sins of pride, lust and idolatry are all intertwined in the beauty battle. Give a current example of how we see these sins working themselves out in beautiful women today.

4. What are some of the false promises of physical beauty? *If you're beautiful, you will be…*

5. Have you fallen for some of these false promises of beauty? Describe your experience.

An Identity Crisis

Dictionary.com defines the word "*identity*" as "the fact of being who or what a person or thing is". Simply put, identity is *who we are*. A popular Christian rap song aptly declares the following truth:

Identity is found in the God we trust
Any other identity will self-destruct

God created us in His image and we were made to find our identity in Him. As we enter into a personal relationship with His Son, Jesus, we become children of God and we are then able to walk in the amazing plan and purpose that we were created for, a life with value and significance that brings glory to our Creator.

John 10:10 puts it this way:

The thief does not come except to steal, and to kill, and to destroy. I have come that they may have life, and that they may have it more abundantly.

We must be able to spot the "identity" lies of our culture. The root of those lies comes as the thief, Satan, seeks to tempt us to find our identity in our physical appearance. Our identity is found in the God who created us, any other identity will self-destruct. Why? Because the beauty battle is a battle against what is good and true and right and beautiful – and our enemy Satan who was prideful in his beauty, went against God. His anger and fury rages on to pervert and destroy God's image in women. Trying to find our identity in the "outer" beauty the world sells will leave a woman empty, disappointed and wounded every time.

Place your trust in the One, Who calls you His masterpiece, the One who has an exciting purpose and plan for your life, the One who loves you with an everlasting love, and the One who has nothing but your best interest at heart. Though the battle continues, you can have a peace in the midst of it as you come to discover the truth of who you were really meant to be.

Today's Beauty Truth

To be truly beautiful is to know that your identity is found in the God who created you.

1. In our image crazed society, how much of what we believe concerning beauty and our identity is based upon what the culture tells us?

2. How do movies, magazines, television, and music affect the way you think about beauty?

3. How does what you see in the media compare with what God's Word says about women and beauty?

4. Look up some verses in the Bible that speak to the issue of beauty.

5. Why is it important that we seek to find our identity in the Word of God versus trying to find it out in the culture?

Beauty: To What Extreme?

Have you ever watched the final tear-jerking moments of *Extreme Makeover*, and felt a bit envious? The latest recipient of a plethora of cosmetic enhancement procedures reveals her new "identity" and walks into a room full of amazed family and friends! We can sympathize with the plights of these candidates who often share tragic life stories of rejection – but though there is a radical makeover on the **outside**, will it take care of the wounds and pain on the **inside**?

Physical beauty doesn't ensure happiness, fulfillment, or success. We can validate this fact by observing the most physically attractive women in the world.

I remember being fascinated with the royal life of Princess Diana. She was the most photographed woman in the world. She became a celebrity of unprecedented magnitude. Yet she lived a troubled life. Her fairy-tale marriage to Prince Charles ended in divorce. Her subsequent relationships with other men all ended unhappily. She admitted to persistent bouts of depression, chronic loneliness, ongoing bulimia and even several suicide attempts. She went to a number of psychotherapists, all to no avail. Her life ended tragically when she was just thirty-six years old.

We see the downward spiral of many a young woman in Hollywood as they walk in the lie that beauty will bring happiness.   Hollywood uses them up and as a last resort they spend their last days of fame on a reality show where they appear brainless and are demeaned by the very fans that cheered for them in the beginning. Their outward beauty quickly fades as they succumb to the ugliness of the lies they have believed in their heart.

Today's Beauty Truth

To be truly beautiful is to recognize our desire for beauty can result in the sin of pride and selfishness.

1. Why are women so obsessed with physical beauty? Why would women go to such extremes to be beautiful as culturally defined? Why aren't we pleased with "normal"?

2. How can our desire for beauty result in the sin of pride and selfishness? Use Scripture to support your answer.

3. How does discontentment play a key role in the beauty battle?

4. Miley Cyrus has caused a stir recently among parents with her participation in the highly provocative song and video, *__Who Owns my Heart__*? Her question is a good one and I believe it reveals her personal struggle – she is being tempted by the lure of the lies about beauty. I picture a tug of war going on as her lyrics describe:

   "I want to believe I'm a masterpiece, but sometimes it's hard in the dark"

   The lies about beauty are dark, and they take us to dark places. Who owns your heart? Why is it so important that God rules and reigns in our hearts?

Week 1
Day 4

Winning the Battle

It is wonderful to know as with every other area of life; God has provided the necessary principles that will help you and me walk in victory as we fight our way through the beauty battle.

There are 4 great truths we see in God's Word that build a strong foundation in a woman's life as she seeks to make wise choices and decisions regarding beauty.

First, recognize that your body does not belong to you, but to God. Your body was meant to glorify Him, to be a living sacrifice, so any time you consider your body and how to treat it, you must consult the Owner.

Second, with a focus on pleasing God, you can make confident choices concerning your appearance. With your identity being anchored in Christ, you can walk in a balanced approach to taking care of yourself and avoid the wrong thinking that tempts you to see beauty as a way to gain worth and value.

Third, God graciously allows you the freedom in Christ to make personal choices, but you are expected to make wise and godly decisions that will distinguish you from the rest of the world. Your freedoms are never to be used in a way that will tarnish your Christian testimony.

Fourth and equally important if not more is that your focus should be on the inner woman. God is looking at your heart. There is nothing wrong with taking care of your outward appearance but when it becomes the issue that drives you, that consumes all of your thinking, time and money; be sure to check your heart and your priorities.

Your greatest source of beauty is a thriving and fruitful relationship with Jesus Christ. A daily diet of His Word and abiding in His presence will change you from the inside out. The beauty that is in your heart will make its way to a glow on the outside that will turn heads wherever you go.

Today's Beauty Truth

To be truly beautiful is to embrace a biblical "beauty" perspective.

Apply it to Your Life

1. Look up and write down the following Scriptures that support what you have read today:

    - 1 Samuel 16:7

    - Romans 8:8

    - 1 Corinthians 6:19-20

    - Titus 2:11-12

    - 1 Peter 3:3-4

2. Which of the above beauty truths most touched your heart and why?

3. How can nurturing your inner beauty benefit your outward beauty?

4. Where do you need victory in the beauty battle? What are some truths from God's Word that can help you to fight back?

5. Are you experiencing a thriving and fruitful relationship with Jesus? Why or why not? Spend sometime in prayer today and ask God to reveal to you anything that may be hindering intimacy and joy in your relationship.

Beauty and the Book of Ephesians

Tucked away in the Book of Ephesians, Chapter 2 verse 10 is the most exalted description of a believer in all of Scripture:

> *For we are God's masterpiece. He has created us anew in Christ Jesus, so we can do the good things he planned for us long ago. (NLT)*

The treasures of Ephesians center on the truth that we are God's masterpiece. **You** are God's masterpiece!

What is a masterpiece?   It is the deepest expression of the artist!! When you listen to a beautiful song, or set your eyes on a beautiful painting, what you're hearing, or what you're seeing, is the deepest expression of who that person is.

And here's the thing that is absolutely fascinating to me about what Paul is saying here: **we are God's deepest expression**. God wants to express Himself, like any other artist would do through their art. You are God's art. You're God's masterpiece. And what does He want to do with you? He wants to express Himself through you.

Masterpiece has been defined as the greatest work of an artist and you are God's greatest work and in the weeks ahead you will come to know, and understand that this is what it means to be "Truly Beautiful."

To be truly beautiful is to know, believe and walk in the truth that you are God's masterpiece. It is to live in the reality that He has created you anew in Christ Jesus so you can enjoy, fulfill and do the good things He planned for you long ago.

As we have learned this week, Satan comes to destroy the masterpiece. Can you imagine someone using a black marker to completely blot out a priceless Picasso or Van Gough? Satan comes to ruin you and to blot out the amazing purpose and plan that God has for your life.

This is why I am sharing the message of "Truly Beautiful". As I have the opportunity to counsel women biblically, I see women experiencing spiritual defeat in their personal lives. That defeat renders them "inactive" for the Kingdom of God. God's plan and purpose for their lives is derailed as they believe lie after lie about beauty. So enough is enough – I am fighting back with the truth. The Book of Ephesians holds the precious truths of who we were meant to be and God's amazing purpose and plan for every believer.

Today's Beauty Truth

To be truly beautiful is to discover who I am in Christ and appropriate those truths in my life.

Apply it to Your Life

1. Some of Paul's most powerful prayers are found in the Book of Ephesians. Read Ephesians 1:15-21 and 3:14-21. What is Paul praying that we would embrace and live out in our lives?

2. God created us with real desires – there are four which we will be looking at throughout our study:

   - The desire to know lasting intimacy and true love
   - The desire to be confident and secure and accepted
   - The desire we have for our lives to have meaning and significance
   - The desire we have to be whole and holy

   Though our desires our valid, they were meant to be satisfied and fulfilled by God. Unless a woman understands who she is in Christ and how to practically live those truths out, she will seek to fulfill these real needs in other ways. These are deeper issues that often get over looked in the battle with beauty.

   Give some examples of how woman can seek to fulfill real needs in the wrong way.

3. Our time together in Ephesians will help us to delve deeply into each one of these four desires teaching us how to live in the purpose and plan God has for our lives and as the masterpieces we were created to be. In which of these four areas are you struggling? Pray and ask God to work in your heart over the next several weeks to give you victory in your personal walk and to move forward in the plan and purpose He has for your life.

Week 2

Daddy's Girl

The search for lasting intimacy and acceptance

Blessed be the God and Father of our Lord Jesus Christ, who has blessed us with every spiritual blessing in the heavenly places in Christ, just as He chose us in Him before the foundation of the world, that we should be holy and without blame before Him in love, having predestined us to adoption as sons by Jesus Christ to Himself, according to the good pleasure of His will, to the praise of the glory of His grace, by which He made us accepted in the Beloved.

Ephesians 1:3-6

You Are My Precious Daughter

You are a daughter of the King, and not just any king. You are *My* daughter, and I am the God of all heaven and earth. I'm delighted with you! You are the apple of my eye. You're Daddy's girl. Your earthly father may love and adore you, but his love is not perfect, no matter how great - or small – it is. Only *My* love is perfect…because *I am love*. I formed your body. I fashioned your mind and soul. I know your personality, and I understand your needs and desires. I see your heartaches and disappointments, and I love you passionately and patiently. My child, I bought you with a price so that we could have an intimate relationship together for all eternity. Soon we will see each other face to face – Father and daughter – and you will experience the wonderful place I have prepared for you in paradise. Until then, fix your eyes on heaven, and walk closely with Me. You will know that – although I am God - My arms are not too big to hold you, my beloved daughter.

Love,

Your King and Your Daddy

in Heaven

Sheri Rose Shepherd

The Father Longing

The supreme revelation of God in the Bible is that He is our Father. The key to knowing you are "Truly Beautiful" is that you are Daddy's girl! Eight times in the Book of Ephesians we are told about our Father. It is a relationship we want to live out and enjoy each and every day. God, your Father, has blessed you with every spiritual blessing in Christ to live in the heavenlies, and where is that - **above** the struggles of every day life.

In 1997 singer and songwriter Bob Carlisle wrote a beautiful ballad called, "Butterfly Kisses". The song describes the tender love between a father and his daughter. It quickly climbed to the top of the charts and received international recognition. In reflecting upon the song's enormous success, Bob Carlisle said this:

"I get a lot of mail from young girls who try to get me to marry their moms. That used to be a real chuckle because it's so cute, but then I realized they don't want a romance for Mom. They want the father that is in that song, and that just kills me."

What these young girls wanted was a daddy…a dad to love them, a dad to protect them, a dad to be kind and tender toward them. They wanted a dad who is strong, dependable and committed – a dad to help them along the way as they grew up, a dad to guide them, a dad to be their greatest fan.

The longing expressed by these young girls is reminiscent of the longing that resides in each of our hearts – to be Daddy's little girl. God has created within our hearts a longing to be fathered by the Father of our dreams, our perfect heavenly Father. The need to be well fathered is a fundamental need of the human heart. It is a need that was put in us by our Creator – the heavenly Father, our true Father – who alone defines what fatherhood means and what fatherhood was meant to be.

Today's Beauty Truth

To be truly beautiful is to know lasting intimacy rests in our relationship to God as our Father.

1. Do you find it difficult to receive the love that your heavenly Father has for you? Why or Why not?

2. Look up three scriptures that speak of God's love for you.

3. Look up the following scriptures and record what you discover about your heavenly Father:

   - Psalm 56:8

   - Isaiah 49:16

   - Matthew 10:30

4. Read the story of the prodigal son in Luke 15:11-32. Write down everything you learn about his father.

5. Have you been running away from God? Even now, the Father's heart is turned toward you. His arms are outstretched waiting for you to return to safety and the comfort of His love. Will you turn your heart toward Him?

Daughter

In Mark chapter 5:25-34, we read about a woman who suffered with an issue of blood for 12 years. Imagine her life, rejected and alone. Society had shunned her and labeled her unclean. She had wasted all of her time, energy and money seeking her healing from the world – which left her not better, but we quickly notice - **only worse**.

She hears about Jesus and by a sheer act of her will comes behind Him in the crowd and touches the hem of His garment. In a moment of complete and utter despair she reaches out with great faith for her healing. Immediately we are told the fountain of her blood is dried up and she felt in her body that she was healed of the affliction. But that is not the end of the story.

Jesus calls her out by asking a question He already had the answer to – "Who touched my clothes"? With fear and trembling she comes out from the crowd falling down before Jesus, sharing the truth of her life with Him. There was probably much sin to confess as a result of the very real pain and agony she had suffered over those twelve long years.

What happens next is crucial to our study today. Jesus responds, "**Daughter**, your faith has made you well. Go in peace, and be healed of your affliction."

Daughter, this endearing, affectionate term, signified her new relationship with Jesus. Her faith had caused her to come to Him, to confess to Him, and He healed her physically and spiritually.

She had placed her trust in Jesus and now became a daughter – adopted into the family, no longer rejected but accepted in the Beloved. We become a daughter of God by faith in His Son, Jesus. We then enjoy a personal relationship with the Creator of the universe! That means we can get to know Him. It means we can talk to him and relate to Him on an intimate basis. We may not completely understand how to relate to an Almighty One, or the Most High, or the Great I Am, because we have no earthly frame of reference to do so, but relating to a father, that's different!

Today's Beauty Truth

To be truly beautiful is to know that you are God's daughter.

1. Sometimes we can have the faulty belief that our heavenly Father is like our earthly father. Even the best father is not perfect like God is. What was your personal relationship with your earthly father like? How has that relationship impacted your relationship with God?

2. Read the story of the woman with the issue of blood in Mark 5:25:34. In what way do you relate to her story?

3. At the root of much of a woman's depression, her self-loathing, and sometimes her hopelessness and despair is the lie that God could not possibly love *her*. Why is it so important that we come to grow in the understanding of God's love for us?

4. As mothers, how can we help our children to know and enjoy a relationship with their heavenly Father?

5. How do we nourish an intimate relationship with God? What things can hinder that intimacy? Use Scripture to support your answer.

Chosen for Relationship

God always takes the initiative in our love relationship. The witness of the entire Bible testifies that God pursues us – that He chose us before the foundation of the world to have a relationship with Him.

What does it mean to be chosen? Webster Dictionary defines chosen in this way, "selected or marked for favor or special privilege or one who is the object of choice or divine favor."

I don't know about you but I always hated those times during P.E. when the team captains got to choose their team members. What a nerve-wracking moment when one by one the more popular students were picked while the less popular prayed they would not be the last one chosen! .

God chose you! Let that sink in. **GOD CHOSE YOU**. He tore Himself away from heaven to come and be with you—the one He loves and chose to be His own to accomplish His purposes in this generation. Before the foundation of the world God had a plan to bring you to Him.

You can have joy, assurance and peace in knowing that God predestined you to be adopted as His child for all eternity and He did this before you were even born! It was His will, His love and great pleasure to choose you!

When you begin to see yourself in the hands of a Father who loved you and chose you personally, it will revolutionize your life. Your fear of rejection is won by your faith in His unfailing love and His promise to never leave or forsake you.

Today's Beauty Truth

To be truly beautiful is to live in the joy and excitement of being chosen.

1. What do you discover as you read John 15:16? What were you chosen for?

2. Continue to search the Scriptures and journal what the Word is revealing to you about being chosen.

   - Deuteronomy 7:6-8

   - 1 Peter 2:9-10

3. Share a time when you experienced rejection. How does it encourage you to know that as one chosen by God, He will never reject you?

4. Consider the words of Charles Spurgeon:

   "Nothing under the gracious influence of the Holy Spirit can make a Christian more holy than the thought that he is chosen. Shall I sin, he says, after God has chosen me? Shall I transgress after such love? Shall I go astray after so much loving kindness and tender mercy? Nay, my God. Since thou hast chosen me, I will love Thee, I will live to Thee, and I will give myself to Thee to be Thine forever, solemnly consecrating myself to Thy service"

   How should the truth that you are chosen impact the way you live?

Abba

Did you know that the Holy Spirit that lives in you is continually crying out Abba, or Daddy? Under the influence of the Holy Spirit, your whole being, heart, mind, soul and strength cries out with an intense longing to connect with your Father. There is a strong and desperate desire for lasting intimacy that calls us and drives us to the Father's heart.

Often we don't recognize the longing. We can't explain why we feel restless or frustrated. Busyness disguises the pain and disappointment we seek to keep under control. We attempt to satisfy our yearnings with substitutes that leave us continually empty.   We go about life on our own forgetting the One who is ready and waiting to fill us with His love and comfort.

It is so important that we recognize the yearnings in our heart when they come, so that we will turn to the One who can satisfy those longings. Are you going ever deeper in your relationship with God? Are you confidently and joyfully entering into His presence? Do you experience His love for you as His daughter? In the difficult times, who do you cry out to?

Intimacy is established in our Father-daughter relationship when we share all of our lives with God. He wants us to run to Him and crawl up in His lap and linger there, to be honest about our sin and share our fears. He longs to bring comfort and healing and address the deep hurts and pains we try to avoid.

Our deepest desire for lasting intimacy will be completely fulfilled when we are finally at home – with our perfect heavenly Father for all of eternity.

Today's Beauty Truth

To be truly beautiful is to recognize my desire for intimacy is only fulfilled in my relationship with God as my Father.

1. Write out Romans 8:15 and share a time in your life when your heart was yearning for intimacy and you reached for a substitute.

2. Read John chapter 15. Write down everything that you learn about abiding.

3. Look up the word "**abide**" in a Bible dictionary. How does the definition help you to better understand the idea of an intimate relationship with God?

4. Is there something right now that you are longing for? What is it? In light of what you have studied today, how will you satisfy that yearning?

5. Read Psalm 63. What do you discover about David's relationship with God?

Week 2
Day 5

Accepted in the Beloved

I love to watch my granddaughter play dress-up. Give her a plastic crown, a pink tutu and a wand and she will instantly become a princess.   Likewise, give a little boy a cap and badge and he will immediately become a police officer. We smile at a child's role playing, but I wonder how much we play dress-up in real life. How often do we pretend to be something or somebody that we really are not?

- We want to belong or be accepted so we dress and act like those we hope will include us.
- We feign interest in things in which we have no interest in order to impress or attract someone.
- We do things we don't want to do just so we can conform to a certain image or expectation.

In addition, we often hide or mask our true thoughts and feelings. We may laugh when we feel like crying, act fearless when we are scared to death, and act like we have it altogether when we're falling apart.

Why do we feel the need to be someone different from who we really are? Why do we feel that we cannot be honest about our true thoughts and feelings? Often it is because of fear. We want to be liked and accepted so it is difficult to be totally, completely transparent with others. We fear people won't like us if they really know us – our weaknesses, insecurities, doubts, and frustrations. It seems easier to pretend to be the person we think they want us to be.

Isn't it wonderful to know that God accepts us just as we are, whether we have it all together or we fail miserably? Did you know that He sees you completed and in glory? ***When He looks at you He sees you covered by the blood of Christ***.

So often we think God is counting our sins as He sees the numbers of times we fail and we blow it, but in reality He is looking at the opportunities we choose to believe Him. Our sins are paid for - past, present and future! To God we are the praise of His glory and it is His good pleasure to accept us into the Beloved.

It was God's plan that the Lord Jesus should first give His life *for* us at Calvary by dying on the cross and then give His life *to* us –when we recognize our need for Jesus and confess our sin and trust Him with our lives – God now sees us in the Beloved and when God looks at us He sees Jesus.

Today's Beauty Truth

To be truly beautiful is to be accepted in the Beloved.

1. God now sees you in the Beloved…to the praise and glory of His grace. God's glory is greatly enhanced by the grace He has shown to us. It was God's idea not ours – we love Him because He first loved us….It was God – your Heavenly Father's plan to seek you out, to save you, to sanctify you and seat you in glory. The endless ages of eternity will prove to be all too short a time to sing His praise for such matchless love and grace.

   Write out the words of 1 John 4:19:

2. We cannot hide from God or pretend to be something we're not because He knows us perfectly. Look up the following Scriptures and note what you discover:

   - Jeremiah 17:10

   - Luke 16:15

   - 2 Timothy 2:19

3. We do not have to worry about whether He will like or accept us. What does His Word assure us of in Romans 8:38-39?

4. God sees in us that which we cannot see in ourselves. We may feel like that preschooler playing dress-up sometimes, like nothing fits us exactly right whether it is our job, home situation, or our lot in life. But God looks past the misfits we feel we are to the individuals that we can become. The Bible is full of examples of ordinary people that He called and equipped for great service, people who didn't always see themselves as God saw them. What woman in the Bible inspires you and why?

5. Read the poem below and journal your thoughts.

   Father, You see me as I am,
   You know me through and through,
   There's nothing within or without
   That I can hide from You.

   Father, such knowledge comforts me,
   For I don't need to pretend,
   I can be honest and open with You,
   You'll always be my friend.

   You see beyond my armor,
   The thick shell I hide within,
   And You peel away each layer
   To let Your light shine in.

   You soften all the hard spots,
   The roughened edges, You smooth,
   You give purpose and direction,
   My tumultuous heart, You soothe.

   You transform this misfit
   Who did not fit in before,
   And You give me life and victory
   I'm not a misfit anymore.

   Journal.

6. You may need to know today that God accepts you. God accepts you, not
   because of anything you have done – but because of the blood of Jesus
   you are accepted in the Beloved. Read 2 Corinthians 5:21 and pray and
   ask God to help you believe and know that you are accepted.

Week 3

The Truth in the Fairy Tale

The Search for True Love

And you *He made alive,* who were dead in trespasses and sins, in which you once walked according to the course of this world, according to the prince of the power of the air, the spirit who now works in the sons of disobedience, among whom also we all once conducted ourselves in the lusts of our flesh, fulfilling the desires of the flesh and of the mind, and were by nature children of wrath, just as the others. But God, who is rich in mercy, because of His great love with which He loved us, even when we were dead in trespasses, made us alive together with Christ (by grace you have been saved), and raised *us* up together, and made *us* sit together in the heavenly *places* in Christ Jesus, that in the ages to come He might show the exceeding riches of His grace in *His* kindness toward us in Christ Jesus. For by grace you have been saved through faith, and that not of yourselves; *it is* the gift of God, not of works, lest anyone should boast. For we are His workmanship, created in Christ Jesus for good works, which God prepared beforehand that we should walk in them.

Ephesians 2:1-10

My Princess

I will protect you

I am your shield of protection. Many times you wonder where I am in the midst of the battle that rages around you. You feel abandoned on the battlefield. Don't be afraid and don't lose faith. I am here, and I am always victorious. I will protect you, but you must trust Me. Sometimes I will lead you to shelter for safety and restoration. Other times I will ask you to join Me on the front line in the heat of the battle. The truth is, I can kill any giant that threatens your life, but, just like David the shepherd boy, it's up to you to march forward, pick up the stones, and face your giant.

I love to prove My strength when the odds are the greatest and hope is smallest. I am truly your shelter and your deliverer – I will protect you no matter where you are.

Love,

Your King and Protector

Sheri Rose Shepherd

Week 3
Day 1

Rich in Grace

What are the dimensions of the grace of God? How extensive are the resources of His grace? So often we drastically underestimate the measure of God's supply of grace for our lives like a little fish thinking the ocean may not be large enough for him.

God is rich in grace. When He forgave our sins, He did so "according to the riches of His grace." Think of the bountiful measure of grace that was bestowed to remove our guilt and shame. God generously poured out His grace in order to wash away our iniquities. When I think of my sin, how deeply grieved I am. We are to be "forgetting those things which are behind", but upon remembrance of our sin we should immediately move from our grief into the glorious deliverance He has provided by His grace. We then move from grief to "joy unspeakable and full of glory."

Yet, in delivering us by His grace He did not deplete the treasures of His grace. In Ephesians 2:7, God speaks of the "exceeding riches of His grace." The Lord's grace is far beyond any richness that we have ever yet comprehended or experienced. God's storehouse of grace is so abundantly full that He will be pouring it out upon us for the "ages to come." Yes, it will take eternity for the Lord to fully demonstrate His grace toward us. This everlasting demonstration of His grace will involve showing His kindness toward all of us who are in Christ Jesus. Think of it — the dimensions of God's grace are sufficient for Him to make us the objects of His kindness forever and ever!

God's grace is like an infinitely vast ocean. Think of the immensity of the oceans of the world. Although they are magnificent in scope, every ocean can be searched out or fathomed. Every ocean has a bottom that can be reached. Though vast, they are finite. Paul testified that the Lord gave him grace to go forth and proclaim the "unsearchable (unfathomable) riches of Christ." There is more grace available in the heart of God for us than there is water in all of the oceans of the world! Truly, no matter how much grace we have already discovered in Christ, we have only begun to search out the riches of His grace toward us. Thus, Peter admonishes us to "grow in grace" and in the knowledge of our Lord and Savior Jesus Christ. So swim "little fish" and explore as much as possible of the ocean of "the riches of His grace."

Today's Beauty Truth

To be truly beautiful is to know and live in the riches of God's grace.

1. Look up the word "grace" in a bible dictionary or concordance and write out some definitions.

2. How has God's grace worked in your life and how is it continuing to work in your life?

3. Share your favorite scripture on grace.

4. How does God's grace enable us to extend grace to others?

5. Why is grace so fundamental to the Christian life? Use Scripture to support your answers.

The Beauty of Brokenness

Our generation has been programmed to pursue happiness, wholeness, good feelings about ourselves, positive self-image, affirmation, and cures for our hurt feelings and damaged psyches. But God is not as interested in these ends as we are. He is more committed to making us holy than making us happy. And there is only one pathway to holiness--one road to genuine revival--and that is the pathway of humility or brokenness.

At first hearing, "brokenness" does not sound like something to be sought after. After all, it seems so negative! We may even be afraid of the concept. Perhaps that is because we have a misconception about the meaning of brokenness. Our idea may be quite different from God's idea. Let me provide you with a definition that I think will help you to better understand it.

Brokenness is that place where we realize that all the things we counted on to make life work, don't. God makes life work. Brokenness often happens when we've crossed over the line of what we can handle on our own, leaving us with nowhere to turn.

Brokenness does not mean, as some think, having a sad, gloomy, downcast countenance -never smiling or laughing. It does not mean always being morbidly introspective. Nor can it be equated with deeply emotional experiences. It is possible to shed buckets full of tears, without ever experiencing a moment of brokenness. Esau cried many tears for trading his birthright for a bowl of stew but he wasn't broken. Further, brokenness is not the same as being deeply hurt by tragic circumstances. A person may have experienced many deep hurts and tragedies, but never have been broken.

Brokenness is not a feeling; rather, it is a choice, an act of the will. It is not primarily a one-time experience or crisis (though there may be crisis points in the process of brokenness); rather, it is an ongoing, continual lifestyle. Many of you experienced "brokenness' when you were saved by Jesus but it is not a one time only condition. Brokenness is a lifestyle of agreeing with God about the true condition of my heart and life, as He sees it. It is a lifestyle of unconditional, absolute surrender of my will to the will of God--a heart attitude that says, "Yes, Lord!" to whatever God says. Brokenness means the shattering of my self-will, so that the life and Spirit of the Lord Jesus may be released through me.

Today's Beauty Truth

To be truly beautiful is a lifestyle of agreeing with God about the true condition of my heart and life, as He sees it.

1. Read Psalm 34:18 and Isaiah 57:15. How do they help you to better understand today's lesson?

2. In our minds broken things lose their value. But God doesn't toss aside broken things. He values them. They are priceless. He remakes them and uses them for His glory. When we are broken, we give to God that which the world views as worthless, and He makes it priceless.

    Share a moment of "brokenness" in your life and how God used it for His glory.

3. Brokenness is my response of humility and obedience to the conviction of the Word and the Spirit of God. And as the conviction is continuous, so must the brokenness be continuous.

    Why is it important that we come to the Word of God with an "attitude of brokenness" before Him? Use Scripture to support your answer.

4. God allows defeat, setback, adversity, or tragedy to bring us to the end of self. In the process He makes us more and more like Christ. What is God allowing in your life right now to bring you to the end of self? Are you cooperating or resisting?

5. True spiritual brokenness is a reflection of a life given to humility and a contrite spirit. Real brokenness is the woman who acknowledges she is no longer her own, she has been bought with a price. Such a woman yields herself to God to be broken and formed into the image of Christ. What are some ways you can develop a lifestyle of brokenness?

Week 3
Day 3

True Love

Ecclesiastes 3:11 tells us that God has made everything beautiful in its time, that He has put eternity in our hearts except that no one can find out the work that God does from beginning to end. He is making us perfectly beautiful. Not one stroke of His hand is out of place or wrong – it is all beautiful. He has placed the desire for true love in our hearts and it is Him and only Him that will fulfill that longing.

1 Corinthians 13 tells us that God's love suffers long and He is kind. He thinks no evil toward you. He is unfailing in His love for you. His love is not imperfect like man's love but perfect. Do you know that God loves you with a perfect love? There is no hint of evil in Him. We often buy into the lie that God is just like us. God is good, perfectly good and His plans are good; they are to prosper you and not to harm you, to give you a hope and a future.

If we believed God's love was true we would not keep returning to a worldly love, only to be disappointed time and time again. We must allow ourselves to bask in God's grace, recognizing at all times our complete and utter need for Him. We must trust His perfect love instead of reaching out for substitutes. If you and I are honest, we would admit that we have often chased after a substitute.

- We have combed the bookstore shelves hoping to help ourselves, of course that book on marriage must have the answer
- We have tuned into Oprah and Dr. Phil hoping to grab some healing there
- We have researched the internet until our fingers are sore – after all knowledge must be the answer
- We have grabbed the alcohol, the drugs, maybe sex and the bad relationship, seeking temporary relief
- We have spent outrageous amounts of money on plastic surgery, this diet – that vitamin – hoping that somehow if we look good on the outside it will heal our problems on the inside
- Maybe we have even gone back to Dr. Religion and the law – certain that if we just do a little more, the healing will come

These cures will leave us disappointed every time. We need to trust the One who created us. The One who knows the beginning from the end, the One who loves us perfectly.

Today's Beauty Truth

To be truly beautiful is to trust the One who loves you perfectly.

Apply it to Your Life

1. Why do you think it is so hard to trust God with your life?

2. What person or circumstance are you having a hard time trusting God for right now?

3. Read Jeremiah 18:1-4. He is the potter and you are the clay. Are you cooperating with God as He seeks to mold you and shape you?

4. Read 1 Corinthians 13:4-8(a) and think about God's love toward you. What do you appreciate about God's love for you?

5. What can you do today to embrace the love of God in your life?

Where is My Prince Charming?

In the fairy tale the beautiful princess always ended up with Prince Charming. Well, what about everybody else? This question cuts deeply to tender, fragile and emotional issues of the heart.

Some of you reading thought you had found that one special relationship. You hoped for it and invested your heart in it only to be disappointed as you watched it crumble in a heap of unfulfilled expectations and broken dreams. Others among you have not yet found that one special person to love and be loved. Others have been married for a while now and somehow the man you wake up with every morning certainly doesn't look like Prince Charming.

The fact is that in human relationships there are few guarantees. They will always have their disappointments, days of regret, and loneliness. Such is the danger of relationships in a fallen world.

But we do see in the Bible promises that lead us to believe that we can trust God to fulfill the deeper need we have for companionship—that of knowing and being known fully by the Ultimate Lover.

Remember that while no one can know you completely, God knows everything about you and loves you anyway. He accepts you just the way you are and He wants to be with you now and forever. He will never abandon you and He is able to meet all of your needs. He is the one special relationship you have been dreaming of all along that will never sour and never disappoint.

As for the beautiful princess that always gets Prince Charming, you are that beautiful princess and you have Jesus to thank for that. He is your Prince Charming and the book of Revelation tells us He will come as our Hero to save the day riding on a white horse!

Today's Beauty Truth

To be truly beautiful is to know that you are a beautiful princess and Jesus is your Prince Charming.

1. Why is it harmful to us to place such high expectations on human relationships? Use Scripture to support your answer.

2. How do the words of Jeremiah 31:3 encourage your heart today?

3. Read Revelation 19:11-16. How should the fact that Jesus is both faithful and true impact the way you live?

4. Read Romans 5:8. What do you discover about the love of God towards you?

5. Take some time and write a love letter to your Prince Charming today!

Worth the Wait

It is a privilege to have this day to share my heart with you. I want to encourage you in your walk of purity and let you know that if you are waiting for the man God has promised you, it will be worth the wait.

If you have compromised your purity, I am here to tell you that the blood of Christ covers sin once you have repented and you can move forward cleansed and pure once again.

I have seen many a "hurt" young woman devastated by a relationship with a man where she gave herself sexually to him only to have him end the relationship. This is not God's design for His daughters. His desire is for a woman to wait until she is married to enjoy the sexual relationship and to experience the beauty of two becoming one flesh. When we give ourselves away prematurely, joining our flesh with that of someone outside the confines of marriage – there is a part of ourselves that we lose. It is painful and goes completely against what God has set aside to be something so very wonderful between a man and a wife.

God is your heavenly Father and the rules He has for living are for your protection and in every boundary He has set up He has your best interest in mind. Will you trust him and wait, knowing it will be worth it?

Next week we will be looking at Ephesians chapter 4. It is the practical outworking of our position in Christ. You are a treasured and valuable possession to God and only a man who loves God and will value the relationship you have with God is worth having. God wants your husband to love you like He loves you and to protect you like He protects you. A man that would interfere in your love relationship with God is not a man that is worth it. One of my prayers for the message of "Truly Beautiful" is that a woman would come to understand her value in Christ and stay true to her resolve to stay pure. And for the woman who has lost her virginity, that she would know God has forgiven her and says to her – "Go and sin no more." Her purity is now in tact.

Today's Beauty Truth

To be truly beautiful is to live pure.

1. How are you doing in the area of your resolve to stay pure? What is your biggest struggle?

2. What precautions can you take as it comes to your resolve to help you in your temptations?

3. If you have confessed your sin of sexual immorality and repented before God, are you walking in the forgiveness that Christ offers you? Why or why not?

4. What does the Bible teach about sexual purity? Record two or three verses that will be helpful to you in the future.

5. Homosexuality is becoming a trend even at the grade school level. How would you counsel a young woman who had been tempted by the sin of homosexuality?

6. Though we are unworthy we must not confuse our unworthiness with our value. Because of God's grace and because we are His, we are valuable, priceless. How does this truth speak to your heart today?

Week 4

The Right Mirror

The Search for Holiness and Wholeness

This I say, therefore, and testify in the Lord, that you should no longer walk as the rest of the Gentiles walk, in the futility of their mind, having their understanding darkened, being alienated from the life of God, because of the ignorance that is in them, because of the blindness of their heart; who, being past feeling, have given themselves over to lewdness, to work all uncleanness with greediness.

But you have not so learned Christ, if indeed you have heard Him and have been taught by Him, as the truth is in Jesus: that you put off, concerning your former conduct, the old man which grows corrupt according to the deceitful lusts, and be renewed in the spirit of your mind, and that you put on the new man which was created according to God, in true righteousness and holiness.

Ephesians 4:17-24

My Princess

Guard Your Mind

I want your mind fixed on Me, my beloved. But I want even more from you. I desire great things for you, so I want you to guard your mind by making an "aware list" – all the things you watch, listen to, and read. Let me show you the things that can carry you away from your calling and destroy your dedication to Me. Even your thoughts can be held captive by the ways of the world. I want to protect you, but I will never force you to listen to My Spirit or make your mind dwell on what is true, pure, and right.

The choice is yours, My love. You **can** have an abundant life, a blessed life – a life of influence for others to follow; or you can join the way of the world. I, your God am asking you today to let your mind dwell on Me and you will discover the kind of life you long to enjoy, not only now, but forever.

Love,

Your King and

Your Peace of Mind

Sheri Rose Shepherd

Week 1
Day 1

The Right Mirror

I think you would agree with me that in order to see ourselves we need a mirror. Imagine how ridiculous it would be to put on our make-up or style our hair without a mirror. We might attempt it and think we look okay but would we really want to risk it? Spiritually, we don't want to risk it either.

As women, one of our biggest problems are the mirrors we use, where and who we look to for a clearer understanding of who we are.

You might recognize some of these mirrors we look into:

- The mirror of our peers
- The mirror of our parents
- The mirror of men
- The mirror of our past
- The mirror of public opinion

Typically it's the mirror of other people's opinions and a desire for their approval – whether it is in our appearance, in our performance or our status – we want that approval.

Think about it, when you were a child, you looked into the mirror of your parents and depending on what you saw – whether your parents were good or bad - you believed what they told you about yourself.

We quickly see that these mirrors, whether our parents or someone else often reflect an image that is not only subjective, distorted and unreliable, but also very changeable. When other people's smiles of approval are replaced by frowns of disapproval, it can quickly lead to guilt, even hostility.

The ideal mirror is the Word of God's love and truth as He has revealed them in His Word. As Christian women we can open our Bible and find on its pages accurate insights into how God views us. His Word reveals His total forgiveness, His perfect and limitless love for us, His constant supply of strength and encouragement and His exciting purposes for our lives. These truths help us to cultivate the image of God in us – and these truths never change.

It's in God's Word that we can find reliable and uplifting truths about ourselves, and dwelling on these truths can produce obedient, confident and joyful living.

Today's Beauty Truth

The only reliable mirror is the mirror of God's Word.

Apply it to Your Life

1. "Mirror, mirror on the wall" – We don't need a magic mirror to tell us how fair we are; the Bible is the only mirror we need. When we look into God's Word, He tells us exactly who we are, what we have, and where we are – we're spiritually beautiful in Christ.

2. Now that you know you are looking in the right mirror, gaze upon your beautiful reflection:

Ephesians 1:4

Ephesians 1:7-8

Ephesians 2:4-5

Ephesians 2:18

Ephesians 3:12

Colossians 1:14

Colossians 1:27

Colossians 2:7

Colossians 2:10

Colossians 2:12

Colossians 2:13

Colossians 3:1-4

3. What mirrors have you been looking into recently that have lied to you?

4. Why is it important that we refuse to look into any other mirror other than God's Word?

5. Are you a people pleaser? Why or why not?

6. Why is the mirror of other people's opinion unreliable?

7. There are five great truths that are ours to live out and embrace that the enemy will seek to tear down. Look up those truths in Scripture and write them out.

- 1 John 1:7

- Romans 6:6

- Galatians 5:16

- Philippians 1:6

- Ephesians 2:10

Now that you have discovered the glorious truth of Scripture, which of these truths do you struggle to believe?

Week 4
Day 2

Cleaning out the Closet

Yes, we are a new creation - but Scripture makes it clear that there is still a pull back to the old life. We must constantly be recognizing and rejecting lies that come from our old self and our old way of living. It is not merely our old actions, but our old outlooks and attitudes that can creep in.

I am sure we can all relate to dirty laundry! We certainly don't want to walk in today what we wore yesterday. **Put off** means to take it off! Paul is using the simplest of terms to illustrate what we must do in the realm of our thought lives and attitudes. We must do this because in reality thoughts become attitudes and attitudes become actions. Putting off thoughts that will reap havoc in our lives will spare us the attitudes and actions that will certainly follow. The same way we throw old clothes out of the closet that don't fit anymore; we throw off our old ways!

Paul says that our former manner of life is corrupt—decayed, dead, foul, selfish, unhappy, and restless. These are the things that have made life unhappy or miserable. He points out that we can recognize these attitudes by the way they operate. They are deceitful lusts. Unfortunately, this word lust is greatly misunderstood in our day. We invariably associate it with something sexual. But this word is much broader than that. It means any urge or basic drive. We will get closer to the essential meaning of this word if we use the term urge. These deceitful urges are constantly coming to us as we react to various situations in which we find ourselves.

The first step in experiencing what God intends for us is to recognize that. Put off the old. That is the first step. The other is to recognize the wonderful possibilities of the new life! If you think about the frustration of trying to change without the Spirit of God, it certainly is a hopeless situation.

But of all human beings, born again Christians have the possibility of doing something entirely different, living by an entirely different principle, because they have been renewed in the attitude of their minds. And that happens in the born again life as the Spirit of God comes into the heart that believes in Jesus Christ. When we believe in Jesus Christ and receive Him as our Lord and Savior, we are renewed in the attitudes of our minds. The new self is in the likeness of God: it is the life of God; it is the image of Jesus Christ; it is His life lived in you. So put on that kind of life, because it is available to you.

Today's Beauty Truth

To be truly beautiful we must put off the old self.

1. Read Ephesians 2:1-3 and list everything you learn about the state of a person before they accept Christ.

1. The following Scriptures give us more insight into this "putting off". What do you learn?

   - Romans 6:6

   - 1 Corinthians 6:9-11

   - Colossians 3:8-10

   - Titus 3:3-5

2. What "old clothes" need to be thrown out of your closet? Why do you keep them there?

3. As we seek to put things off we must include guilt, shame and condemnation and understand that Jesus said, "It is finished." We must believe we are who God says we are and leave it at that.

   Write out the truth of Romans 10:11:

   To think about:

   As we continue on our sin no longer defines who we are – it refines who we are. Our position never changes and each and every day we look a little more like Jesus.

Week 4
Day 3

A New Wardrobe

If you are anything like me you have experienced one of those frustrating "I don't have anything to wear" moments. It may have been a wedding or a holiday party or other special occasion that prompted you to try on everything in your closet only to discover that you must have something "new". What's in the closet will just not do!

You might laugh but that is really what Ephesians chapter 4 is talking about – it has the idea of putting off a set of clothes. Think of a prisoner who is released from prison, but still wearing his prison clothes, acting like a prisoner and not a free man. The first thing you would tell him is go put on some new clothes!

So it should be with our new lives in Christ. Anything other than Christ-like character and attitudes will not do! We have not so learned Christ – in other words, we know better. Even as putting on different clothes will change the way we think about ourselves and see ourselves, even so putting on different conduct will start to change our attitudes. This means that we shouldn't wait to feel like the new woman before we put on the new woman.

You have not so learned Christ: The repetition of this idea shows that putting on the new woman has a strong aspect of learning and education to it. You have heard Him and have been taught by Him, as the truth is in Jesus. Our Christian life must go beyond head knowledge, but it must absolutely include head knowledge and affect our whole manner of thinking. Not just in the sense of knowing facts, but the ability to set our minds on the right things.

The Ephesians learned Christ, not only learning about Jesus, but also learning Him. This means a living, abiding knowledge of Jesus will keep us from living in our old sinful conduct. Just knowing about Jesus isn't enough to keep us pure. Spurgeon said it this way:

"So, if you want to know the Lord Jesus Christ, you must live with Him. First He must Himself speak to you, and afterwards you must abide in Him. He must be the choice Companion of your morning hours, He must be with you throughout the day, and with Him you must also close the night; and as often as you may wake during the night, you must say, 'When I awake, I am still with thee.'" (Spurgeon)

Apply it to Your Life

1. The book of Romans wonderfully outlines the spiritual makeover that happens when each person accepts Jesus Christ as Lord and Savior. Look up and record the following verses.

   - Romans 3:23-24

   - Romans 5:8

   - Romans 6:23

   - Romans 8:1

   - Romans 10:9-10

   - Romans 10:13

2. Read Ephesians 4:20-22 in the "Message". How does this help you to better understand today's lesson?

3. Read Galatians 5:22-26. The fruits of the Spirit are a good way to measure if God's Word and His Holy Spirit are changing you. Are you growing in these fruits? Why or why not?

4. Colossians 3:12-17 tells us what to add to our new wardrobe. What new clothes will you be wearing? How will they attract others?

An Inside Job

So many of us want to make changes in our lives but definitely go about it the wrong way. The word "transformed" in the Bible (Romans 12:2) is the Greek word, "*metamorphoo*" which comes from metamorphosis. Picture the process of the transformation of a worm to a butterfly.

God's Word actually instructs us to be "morphed" or changed. This single word provides the key for understanding how spiritual transformation occurs. It directly challenges our ideas about trying harder to live holy lives. It emphasizes God's power and participation. Our way leads to frustration, failure and disappointment, but God's way leads to metamorphosis, a changed life. Just as God miraculously supernaturally turns a caterpillar into a beautiful butterfly, so He supernaturally transforms us into a new creation.

Transformation is not a switching from the to-do list of the flesh to the to-do list of the law. In Galatians 5, when Paul replaces the list of the works of the flesh, he does not replace it with the works of the law but the fruit of the Spirit! The Christian alternative to immoral behaviors is not a new list of moral behaviors. Instead of trying to be good we need to rely on and rest in God changing us.

It is the triumphant power and transformation of the Holy Spirit through faith in Jesus Christ—our Savior, our Lord, and the supernatural power of the Word of God that changes us from the inside out!

Paul uses an amazing phrase in Ephesians 4:23 that parallels this thought. He says, "Be renewed in the spirit of your minds." Now what in the world is that? Our minds have a spirit, a bent, a mindset that is hostile to the absolute Lordship of Christ in our lives. This is where a woman's selfish desire for beauty comes from. She sees herself more worthy of praise. She attributes her achievements to her own efforts. Her mindset is normally, it's all about me!

The battle of beauty begins in our minds. Because the battle begins in the mind it is important that we change the way we think, so we can change the way we live.

Today's Beauty Truth

To be truly beautiful is to be transformed by the renewing of our mind.

1. How does the truth of Romans 12:1-2 support what you learned in today's passage?

2. As we worship God with our lives we must understand that worship that pleases God is informed, rational and intelligent. It is offered by the Christian who understands who God is, what He has given us in the gospel, and what He demands from us.

   Read Archbishop William Temple of Canterbury's enlightening definition of worship:

   Worship is the submission of all of our nature to God. It is the quickening of conscience by His holiness, nourishment of mind by His truth, purifying of imagination by His beauty, opening of the heart to His love, submission of will to His purpose, and all this gathered up in adoration is the greatest of human expressions of which we are capable.

   What does Archbishop Temple mean when he defines worship as "the nourishment of the mind by God's truth"?

3. How are you nourishing your mind to the truths of God's Word?

4. No more stinkin' thinkin'. Read Romans 8:5-8 and record everything you learn about the mind that thinks according to the Spirit and the mind that thinks according to the flesh.

5. Read Philippians 4:8 and make a list of what we are to think about. Beside each entry, write a word that represents the opposite thought. On a scale of one to ten, with ten being the positive thoughts and zero being the negative thoughts, how would you judge your thinking?

The Beauty of Holiness

It is frightening to think and altogether true that words like "discretion," "holiness," "modesty" and "purity" are disappearing from our world's vocabulary. In a culture that is rapidly declining morally, it is easy to become desensitized to the idea of walking in holiness and what it really means.

Holiness on a larger scale implies fidelity – fidelity to God and His Word. The new woman was created in God's image, in true righteousness and holiness. She is the person created in the image of God and her position in Christ is to be worked out practically in her life.

Limiting the definition of holiness to certain areas of the Christian life actually does more harm than good. We want to embrace holiness as faithfulness to Christi. When we understand that the boundaries for living that God places in His Word are for our protection, we appreciate the quality of life that obedience to the Word of God brings.

Holiness is not something we do – it is what Jesus did for us. God sees you as holy, covered by the blood of Christ. But this truth should set us free to be who we really are and motivate us to live that way – set apart. A set apart life is a beautiful life. It is a life that attracts others to it. A woman who knows who she is in Christ and walks in the fullness of that knowledge radiates and communicates a beauty that is not seen in the world. The lure of that beauty is not fleshly, it is spiritual and it brings forth eternal fruit.

Whether it is the way we dress, the way we speak, the movies we choose to watch or waiting until we are married to have sex, it all comes from a heart that loves God and desires to be faithful to Him. It is a heart that is grateful and understands the high price that Jesus paid by going to the cross. It is a heart that values a redeemed life.

This is a heart that is engaged in relationship – not duty – a heart that so loves the One who has saved her that she can do nothing else but be faithful to Him and to live to please Him.

That is the attitude of holiness. Have you ever had someone tell you that you looked like Jesus? That is perhaps the greatest statement we could ever hope to hear – that we are walking in the light – that the character traits that won people to Jesus are alive and well in us. Oh how women today that don't know Christ need to see holiness in our lives.

Today's Beauty Truth

To be truly beautiful is to live a lifestyle of holiness.

Apply it in Your Life

1. Look up the word "holiness" in a Bible dictionary and journal the definitions that help you to better understand it.

2. Why is it important to recognize that holiness should invade our entire life?

3. Read 2 Corinthians 7:1. How does this passage build upon what you are learning today?

4. Write out the words of Psalm 29:2. What does it mean to worship the Lord in the beauty of holiness?

5. Have you discovered that the boundaries God has for our lives are for our protection? Why or Why not? What happens when we step out of those boundaries?

6. Find two or three Scriptures today that can help you as you seek to walk in an attitude of holiness.

Week 5

His Masterpiece

The Search for Confidence and Significance

For we are God's masterpiece.
He has created us anew in Christ Jesus,
so we can do the good things he planned for us long ago.

Ephesians 2:10 (NLT)

You Are My Masterpiece

I love what I have created. I am delighted in you!

Don't ever feel insecure about what you think you are not, because I made you in my image and your uniqueness is a gift from Me. I did not give you a life, My love, for you to squeeze into a man-made mold. You are royalty, but you won't discover that truth by gazing into a mirror. Let Me be your mirror and I will reflect back to you your true beauty. The more you gaze at Me, the more you will see my workmanship in you. The sooner you see yourself for who you really are, the sooner you begin your reign as My priceless princess with a purpose.

Love,

Your King and Your Creator

Sheri Rose Shepherd

Week 5
Day 1

One of a Kind

God created each of us uniquely and we are "truly beautiful" just the way He made us. Psalm 139:13-16 tells us how we are to think about ourselves:

> *For You formed my inward parts; You covered me in my mother's womb. I will praise You, for I am fearfully and wonderfully made; Marvelous are Your works, and that my soul knows very well. My frame was not hidden from You, when I was made in secret, and skillfully wrought in the lowest parts of the earth. Your eyes saw my substance, being yet unformed. And in Your book they all were written, the days fashioned for me, when as yet there were none of them.*

Each of us is irreplaceable…one of a kind…priceless! And sometimes I wonder if it isn't like a slap in God's face when we are disappointed in who He made us to be or wanting to be someone else.

In C.S. Lewis'. "Voyage of the Dawntreader", Lucy has discovered the Book of Incantations. A green mist forms behind her as she begins to read:

> An infallible spell to make you she –
> the beauty you've always wanted to be."

The book becomes a mirror and she sees her sister Susan. Realizing the spell has turned her into her sister, she says, "I'm beautiful." Lucy's desire is temporarily granted and she quickly finds herself in a world without Lucy. She begins to panic as pieces of her life begin to disappear. Aslan enters the scene and asks, *"What have you done, child? You wished yourself away and with it much more."*

How about you, are you wishing yourself away? We can be just like Lucy, tempted to want to be someone else, longing for their life instead of our own. Think about that seriously for a moment. Who in your world is looking to you to lead the way: If you decided to be someone else who would miss out on what *your* life brings?

God has an amazing plan and purpose for you – that no one else can fulfill but *you*. He has uniquely gifted *you* for what it is that He has created *you* to do! When *you* begin to walk in the works that He has planned for *you*, when *you* begin to embrace the way He has made *you*, you will discover a passion for life that you never had before!

Today's Beauty Truth

You are one of a kind. No one else can take your place.

Apply it to Your Life

In our worst moments, we wonder about our purpose, our value, and our significance. In those moments, let's look at the beautiful universe God has created and then push back the voice of Satan who is trying to make us feel valueless and hear the voice of God, "You are my masterpiece, created to bring a blessing to others."

1. Masterpiece has been defined as the greatest work of an artist and you are God's greatest work. Do you think of yourself as God's greatest work? Why or why not?

2. Why is understanding that we are God's masterpiece vital to a victorious walk with Christ? Use Scripture to support your answer.

3. Think of the most spectacular sunset setting against the backdrop of His vast ocean and know this - creation was not His ultimate workmanship - **you** are. Read Romans 12:3 – how should we see ourselves?

To Ponder:

In Christ we are of untold worth. This great truth may be hard to actually take hold of as we exist in frail human bodies carried along in the rush of modern day busyness. Some of us have had things happen which make us doubt our worth. But we are His workmanship – His work of art – moreover we are in process. Michaelangelo was once asked what he was doing as he chipped away at a shapeless work – He replied, "I am liberating an angel from this stone." – that's what God is doing with us – we are in the hands of the Great Maker – the ultimate Sculptor who created the universe out of nothing, and he has never yet thrown away a rock on which He has begun a masterwork.

But even though we are in process we must have faith to believe what God already sees – we are that completed masterpiece now – God will be faithful to complete His work in you. He is already doing that now through His Word, His Holy Spirit and everything that happens to you is another beautiful brush on the canvas.

Remember, you are God's special treasure, selected by Him and for Him. You are created in the image of Almighty God. He made you exactly the way He intended, and He equipped you with everything you need. You have the strength to stand strong in the midst of difficult situations and the wisdom it takes to make good decisions. Understanding exactly whose you are, and how you fit-in God's plan creates such purpose, confidence and such identity. You have an assignment and you are full of gifts, talents, encouragement and love. You have rich treasure inside you that people need. You have the power of Christ living in you to accomplish more than you ever thought possible. Dare to be bold in your calling because the time grows short…

Journal your thoughts to share…

Week 5
Day 2

A Life of Significance

In a conversation from Alice in Wonderland, Alice asks the Cheshire Cat, "Would you tell me, please, which way I ought to go from here?" "That depends a good deal on where you want to get to," said the Cat. "I don't much care where," said Alice. "Then it doesn't matter which way you go," said the Cat.

Our lives are not to be aimless. God has a plan and purpose for your life that only you can fulfill. Christ-likeness and Christ's glory gives purpose to every believer's life. God's Word teaches us how to live like Christ. As we begin to resemble Christ, we become aware of how He made us; we begin to discover the gifts He has given us to bring Him glory. As we understand and receive His love, we are then able to share it in the spheres of influence where He has placed us.

As we discover how He has made us and the gifts He has blessed us with we are able to bring a focus to our lives. His unique purpose for us will determine how we spend our time, energy and resources. When we discover what we were made to do – we will wake up every morning eager and excited to play a part in His kingdom plan. What God has created us to do, we love to do and we never grow weary of doing it.

I remember the day God placed a passion in my heart for women's ministry. The funny thing about it was the church I was attending didn't have a women's ministry! At that same time I met the woman who would take me to my first women's conference. She mentored me, helped me to identify my gifts and focus on the plan and purpose God had for my life. I experienced such joy and excitement in that season of my life as I recognized my purpose. It allowed me in the years to come to say yes to the things that mattered and no to the things that would distract me.

Eighteen years later, I am still passionate about women's ministry and God has grown me in both my Christ-likeness and my gifting. I have grown in my gifts of teaching and writing. He has also expanded my sphere of influence. A few years ago God brought me to a ministry of biblical counseling. This is something I had never imagined. As we begin to walk in the purpose and plan that God has for our lives, He will be faithful to lead us. If our hearts desire is to bring Him glory and if we yield to His perfect plan, we will live lives of eternal significance. That desire in our heart to make a difference in the world will be satisfied as we step into all that God has for us!

Today's Beauty Truth

To be truly beautiful is to walk in the purpose and plan that God has for your life.

Apply it to Your Life

1. What are some ways we can discover God's plan and purpose for our lives. Use Scripture to support your answer.

2. There are three reasons why it is important to know your spiritual gifts:

   - Knowing your spiritual gifts will enable you to find your place of ministry in the local church.
   - Knowing your spiritual gifts will enable you to determine your priorities.
   - Knowing your spiritual gifts will be of great help in discerning God's will.

   What do you have a passion for? Have you identified any of your spiritual gifts? Why or why not?

3. Read 1 Corinthians 12:1-11 and Romans 12:3-8. What are some of the spiritual gifts God gives to believers? What are some other things you learn from these passages?

4. Write out 1 Peter 4:10. How does this Scripture build upon today's lesson?

5. We have a great God! Share a God-sized dream and don't be afraid to believe God for it! Have your friends join you in prayer – if your heart and motive is to bring God glory, He can make it happen!

God Confidence

Are you surprised to learn that some of the great leaders in Scripture struggled with the same feelings of inadequacy that you do? I am certainly encouraged to know that I am not alone in believing I can't do something. What is the real problem with this kind of thinking? I am looking at myself and comparing myself to the task to which God has called me. No wonder I feel inadequate. I am inadequate.

Yet God does not call me to do anything for Him out of my own resources. He calls me to be faithful and to allow Him to work through me. Yes, this involves stepping out in faith. Yes, this is scary. Yes, I don't always know the entire plan or the outcome. But He is always faithful.

We see Moses' reluctance to answer the call of God yet this is the same man who stood before Pharaoh and who led the children of Israel as they crossed the Red Sea. Just as God gave Moses what he needed to be the leader and the deliverer of the children of Israel, we have been given what we need to accomplish the task God has assigned us to.

Paul said that he "put no confidence in the flesh" (Philippians 3:3). In other words, he didn't think that he was good enough because of any particular talent or ability that he had on his own. But his confidence came from his understanding of who he was as a child of God. Someone once said, "A man wrapped up in himself makes a pretty small package. But a man, or woman, wrapped up in God is an amazing sight to behold."

Confidence in God empowers us, energizes us, and strengthens us. It is this confidence in God that is going to make it possible to achieve and accomplish anything and everything that God the Father sets out before us. Confidence in God drives out fear, doubt, anxiety, and worry, allowing us to make an impact in the world for Him.

God confidence believes that I am His masterpiece! He has created me for a purpose and plan that has eternal implications. He will supply all that I need to walk forward in that calling, but I must have faith to take the first step!

Today's Beauty Truth

To be truly beautiful is to be confident in an amazing God and His plan and purpose for my life!

1. Moses had asked, "Who am I?" implying his complete inadequacy for his calling. In Exodus 3:14 God replied, "I am who I am!" implying His complete adequacy. The issue was not who Moses was but who God is. Can you identify with Moses and with his feelings of inadequacy? What are some areas in which God might want to use you, but in which you are holding back, perhaps out of fear?

2. Read Jeremiah 1:4-8. How did Jeremiah feel when God called him to be a prophet? What were his hesitations? How did God answer him?

3. What is the difference between self-confidence and God-confidence? Why is this important?

4. Perhaps you are reluctant to follow God. What do the following verses, written to those seeking to trust God, tell you that might help you and encourage you to be God-confident?

    Philippians 1:6

    Philippians 3:4-9

    Philippians 4:13

    2 Timothy 1:7

If you struggle with feeling inadequate, confess to the Lord that you are focusing on yourself and your resources instead of on Him and His resources. Write a prayer asking God to help you remember to choose to be God-confident instead of self-confident. Thank Him for being the all-sufficient God!

Week 5
Day 4

God's Plan for all Women

Perhaps there is nothing as beautiful in the Word of God as His plan for women as they age and mature. In Chapter 2 of Titus, God issues His mandate for women – older women are instructed to train the younger women in godly living, so that a legacy will be established for succeeding generations.

God wants each generation to know Him personally and have the joy of living an abundant life full of purpose and fruitfulness. He wants the world to know that living life His way works because He loves us and wants our best. Not only that, He wants His daughters to walk in obedience so that His Word is not dishonored.

A Titus 2 woman is not meant to be an inspirational picture of virtuous women from long ago. Actually it is quite the opposite. God's Word presents the Titus 2 woman as God's plan, God's desire, and God's marching orders for all women in Christ of any age in any era.

What does she look like today? The Titus 2 woman is saved by grace, and energized by the Spirit of God to live such an extraordinary life that the world, her husband, and her children all notice that she is different because she is in step with the Spirit and Word of God. As the Titus 2 woman ages, she becomes more beautiful and more fruitful. Her life is marked by her love for God and His Word. She finds her strength in His endless grace and is able to live each day in the Lord.

If married, she is a wife who loves her husband in such a profound way that he is deeply satisfied in her love; and if she is a mother, her children know they are deeply loved. Whether single or married, mother, wife, or alone; she is a woman that over the long haul radiates love, contentment, peace, and joy.

Age alone, however, does not qualify an older woman to leave a godly legacy. Titus outlines character qualities that define who this older woman is to be in order for her to train young women. The commission to train the younger generation of women is given to older, mature Christian women who have faithfully built into their own lives the message they are to impart to others.

Today's Beauty Truth

To be truly beautiful is to walk in the fullness and fruitfulness of the Titus 2 model.

Apply it to Your Life

Being a leader in women's ministry and a pastor's wife, I have the opportunity to meet with women ministry directors from all over the area and encourage them in the work of the Lord. Many are struggling with keeping their mentoring ministries available to the body. It is not for a lack of young women mentees – there are not enough mentors to go around. Unfortunately older women often fall into a faulty mindset that "they have done their time" or they feel they have nothing to offer. Many feel they have nothing in common with younger women. Of course we know that this reasoning is not at all biblical.

1. Write Titus 2:3-5. How does this biblical mandate counter the above arguments about older women?

2. Titus 2:3-5 outlines character qualities that define who an older woman is to be in order for her to train young women. What are the five character qualities of the Titus 2 woman?

3. How old is old? Certainly the 20 something who loves God and His Word has something to offer someone younger. Give an example of opportunities for "younger women" to serve in Titus roles.

4. Have you believed the lie that you have nothing to offer a woman younger than yourself? Why or why not?

5. How does busyness hinder the progress of Titus 2 ministry?

The Beauty of a Titus 2 Woman

As we come to the end of our "Truly Beautiful" study perhaps there is nothing more beautiful than the Titus 2 woman who is reverent in her behavior and a teacher of good things. She sees life, all of life, from God's viewpoint and she understands that even the mundane routines of life are important to God. Her lifestyle tells a watchful observer where her priorities are. If you were to watch her throughout her day, you would discover that she walks very closely to God. Her actions clearly flow from a heart that desires to live for God. Her life revolves around things that matter to Him.

How did she arrive at this place in her life? She has kept and continues to keep her relationship with God first. He is her first love and her first priority. God's Word is her source of truth and as she abides in relationship with Him, His power is continually available to her.

The woman who is reverent in her behavior and a teacher of good things consistently spends time studying God's Word, in order to stay in communion with the Father. She understands that the Word of God is the foundation for understanding God's character, His will, and what pleases Him. The reverent woman fears God, walking by faith in obedience to His Word. Her choices and decisions are godly, based on her respect and trust in God and His ways and she is able to teach others what she has learned.

It is impossible to be a woman who is reverent in her behavior without the foundation of God's Word, and without a choice to obey God by faith. Over time, the woman who consistently responds in obedience to God's principles will become mature. A mature woman possesses a "God consciousness" that influences her daily regimen. She evaluates every thought, action, and encounter by the standard of the Bible. Truth lights her path so that she can choose obedient behavior which is an outward expression of a heart that knows and communes with the Father.

Simply put, the woman who is reverent in her behavior and a teacher of good things is passionately in love with her Savior; her reverence, or "God-fearing" behavior, flows from a cultivated heart-life with the Father. She loves the truth of the Bible, not as an end in itself, but as a vehicle which leads her into intimate communication with her Father. She understands who God is, and goes heart-to-heart to keep the fine edge of her walk with God sharply honed.

Today's Beauty Truth

To be truly beautiful is to continue to grow more beautiful everyday in your walk with Christ.

Apply it to Your Life

1. Knowing God's Word is key to both reverent behavior and the wisdom to be a teacher of good things. Note the principle from each of the following verses that supports a woman in her desire to be a Titus 2 model.

   - Psalm 119:105

   - Proverbs 9:10

   - Romans 10:17

   - Romans 14:23 (b)

   - 2 Corinthians 10:3-5

   - 2 Timothy 2:15

   - Hebrews 4:12

   - Hebrews 11:6

   - James 1:22

2. Why is it so important that a Titus 2 woman understand the message of "Truly Beautiful"?

3. Comment on the following statement: "Mature women in Christ do not become conformed to His image by accident."

4. What are you doing to develop the disciplines of godliness? What one thing could you begin to do this week that would build your relationship with God?

5. Read 2 Peter 1:3-8. What has God provided for you?

6. What woman has had a great spiritual impact on your life? What personal qualities does she possess that inspire you to have a greater desire to become like Christ?

7. Share three ways God has worked in your life through your "Truly Beautiful" study.

I would love to hear how the "Truly Beautiful" study encouraged you. Please feel free to send me an e-mail at mhill@wmconnection.org

You are Truly Beautiful

About the Author

Margy Hill's passion and calling for women's ministry led her to start the Women's Ministry Connection where she encourages and exhorts women leaders in ministry. God has given her the opportunity to speak into the lives of women of all ages and church backgrounds.

She loves to teach and share her passion for the Word of God to stir women to a deeper and more abundant relationship with Jesus and to encourage and equip them to walk in the fullness of their callings.

Her gift for writing has led her to write several Bible studies to help women develop a desire to dig deeper into the Word of God. With challenging questions and everyday application, her studies have been widely used throughout churches in the United States.

Margy speaks and teaches for women's conferences, retreats and seminars and is also known for her "Hope for the Hurting Heart" training seminars to help equip women to counsel confidently from the Word of God.

For more information, visit her website at www.wmconnection.org.

Made in the USA
Charleston, SC
17 September 2013